PUPPET PLAY

The Ugly Duckling

Moira Butterfield

Heinemann
LIBRARY

First published in Great Britain in 1998 by Heinemann Library,
Halley Court, Jordan Hill, Oxford, OX2 8EJ,
a division of Reed Educational & Professional Publishing Ltd.
Heinemann is a registered trademark of Reed Educational & Professional Publishing Ltd.

OXFORD FLORENCE PRAGUE MADRID ATHENS
MELBOURNE AUCKLAND KUALA LUMPUR SINGAPORE TOKYO
IBADAN NAIROBI KAMPALA JOHANNESBURG GABORONE
PORTSMOUTH NH CHICAGO MEXICO CITY SAO PAULO

Editor: Alyson Jones
Designer: Joanna Hinton-Malivoire
Illustrator: Woody
Printed and bound in Italy.

02 01 00 99 98
10 9 8 7 6 5 4 3 2 1

British Library Cataloguing in Publication Data
Butterfield, Moira
   The ugly duckling - (Puppet play)
   1. Tales - Juvenile drama 2. Ugliness - Juvenile drama
   3. Children's plays, English 4. Puppets - Juvenile literature
   I. Title 822.9'14

ISBN 0 431 03479 6 (Hardback)
   0 431 03483 4 (Paperback)

You will need scissors and craft glue to make
the puppets and props for your play. Always
make sure an adult is there to help you.

CONTENTS

THE STORY OF THE UGLY DUCKLING

A mean dog, cat and chicken tease
the ugly duckling. Now you can make
some spoon puppets to act out
their story and discover how the
duckling surprises all the animals!

READING THE PLAY

Here are the puppet characters in this play:

The duckling babies
Always teasing and jeering

The Ugly Duckling
A sad little bird

The dog, cat and chicken
Three mean farm animals

Sometimes the
puppeteer speaks.
That's the person who
works the puppets.

Do this part in
an ordinary voice.

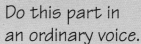

If you want to perform this
story as a puppet show
there are some tips for
you on pages 6-9.

If you prefer, ignore the
stage directions and read
the play with a friend. Share
out the parts between you.

The play is split up into parts. Next to each part there is a name so you know who should be speaking.

They're right. I'm too ugly to show my face anywhere. I'll go and live all on my own.

Ugly duckling

Sometimes there are stage directions. They are suggestions for things you might get your puppets to do at a performance.

Make crying and sniffing noises. Then put up the clump of weeds.

Making Puppets

What you need

* Card
* Paint, coloured paper or fabric
* Wooden spoons
* Scissors & pencil
* Plant stick
* Glue and sticky tape

1 First design your puppet on paper. Then draw on card the head and body parts to be stuck onto the spoon.

2 Glue all the shapes onto the back of the spoon. Decorate the puppet with paint, or glue on coloured paper or fabric.

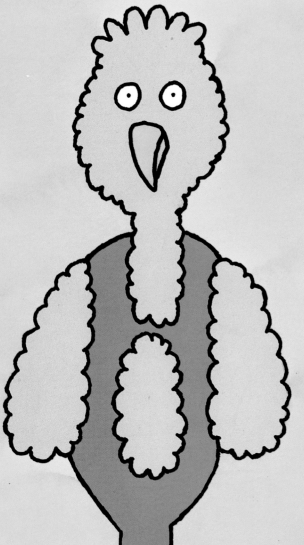

Ugly duckling

Stick some cotton wool on the chest. Add some coloured paper wing feathers.

6

SWAN

Glue a card eye and beak to the back of the spoon. Then wrap some paper round the spoon, glue it in place and cut it into a wing shape.

DUCKLING BABIES

Draw three duckling babies on card and cut them out. Paint them or stick coloured paper eyes and beaks on. Then tape them onto a stick.

DOG, CAT AND CHICKEN

Make a cat, dog and chicken spoon puppet, gluing on card shapes and decorating as shown.

To work a puppet, hold it at the bottom of the spoon or stick. Make sure your hand stays hidden.

MAKING PROPS

WHAT YOU NEED

* Scissors and pencil
* Plant sticks
* Card
* Glue and sticky tape
* Pens or paints to decorate each prop
* Hand mirror
* White paper or desiccated coconut

EGG

1 Draw a large egg shape on card and cut it out. Draw a zig-zag line 4cm from the top. Cut along the zig-zag.

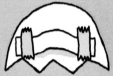

2 Tape a strip of card to the back of the top piece. Make it big enough to fit over the ugly duckling's head.

3 Tape a stick to the bottom piece of the egg.

Hold the ugly duckling puppet behind the egg. Move the spoon up as if the duckling has just hatched from the egg.

FLYING SWANS

Tape some flying swan shapes to a stick and decorate them.

CLUMP OF WEEDS

Tape this card shape to a stick and colour it green.

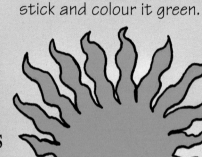

POND AND SNOW

Keep a hand mirror ready as the pond that the ugly duckling looks into. For snow try a handful of desiccated coconut or tiny pieces of torn-up white paper. Remember to clear up afterwards.

MAKING A THEATRE

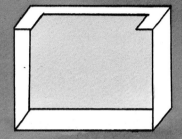 

1 Cut the two bumper packets as shown. Tape back any strips that fall off and tape all the joints to make them secure.

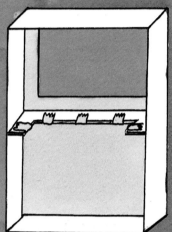

2 Glue the two together as shown and add some tape too, to make the join really strong. Glue and tape a medium-sized box to each side to help your theatre stand up.

3 Decorate the theatre with coloured paper or paints. Stick extra card shapes on if you like, such as a pointed top.

4 Stand the theatre on a table so you can comfortably hide behind it with your puppets and book. Prop the book inside, or lay it flat on the table. Then practise before you invite an audience to watch your play.

THE UGLY DUCKLING

Put your head up to speak to the audience.

Puppeteer

Hello everyone. Do you ever tease people who look different to you? If you watch my play you'll find out why that's a bad idea.

Hide yourself below the stage. Hold the bottom half of your egg prop on stage. Hold the ugly duckling puppet behind it, with the top half of the egg on his head.

Puppeteer

Once upon a time a mother duck was looking after a clutch of eggs. One was much bigger than the others and it took longer to hatch.

Speak from below the stage. Lift the ugly duckling puppet so it hatches.

Puppeteer: Out came a very ugly duckling.

Ugly duckling: Quack, quack!

Take away the egg and ugly duckling. Now show the line of babies with the ugly duckling following behind.

Puppeteer: The other babies were not very nice to the ugly duckling.

11

Shake the babies when they are talking. Shake the ugly duckling when he is talking.

Babies

Why are you so much bigger than us?

Ugly duckling

I don't know.

Babies

Why are you so much uglier, too?

Ugly duckling

Am I?

Babies

Of course you are. Ugly, ugly! Go away, ugly!

Take the babies away, leaving the ugly duckling on his own.

Ugly duckling

Nobody wants me here. I'm just too ugly. I'll run away so they won't have to see my face any more.

Make crying and sniffing noises and move the ugly duckling across the stage, as if he's waddling along.

13

Put up the dog puppet.

Dog: Woof! This is my farm, What do you want?

Ugly duckling: I'm looking for a new home.

Dog: You're very ugly. Can you herd sheep?

Ugly duckling: No, but I can swim.

Dog: That's no good.
You can't stay here.

Put the dog down. Move the ugly duckling along and stick the cat up.

Cat

Meow. This is my garden. What do you want?

Ugly duckling

I'm looking for a new home.

Cat

You're rather ugly. Can you catch mice?

Ugly duckling

No, but I can quack.

Cat

That's no use. You can't stay here.

Put the cat down. Move the ugly duckling along and stick the chicken up.

Chicken

Cluck, cluck. This is my field. What do you want?

Ugly duckling

I'm looking for a new home.

Chicken

You're the ugliest bird I've ever seen. Can you lay an egg every morning?

Ugly duckling

No. I just swim and quack.

Chicken

Stupid ugly bird. Go away!

Take the chicken away, leaving the ugly duckling on his own.

They're right. I'm too ugly to show my face anywhere. I'll go and live all on my own.

Ugly duckling

Make crying and sniffing noises. Then put up the clump of weeds.

Put the ugly duckling behind the clump of weeds. Hold the two together with one hand so you have another hand free.

Ugly duckling

I'll hide in this clump of weeds. Nobody will have to see me ever again. I'll just stay here out of the way.

Make two small sad quacks.

18

Speak from below the stage.

Soon winter came. Snow fell on the ugly duckling and he nearly froze.

Puppeteer

Throw your paper or coconut snow on stage.

Icy winds blew through his feathers.

Puppeteer

Make the sound of a fierce wind and shake the clump of weeds and the ugly duckling.

Take down the ugly duckling puppet from behind the clump of weeds. Replace him with the swan puppet.

Puppeteer

At last winter came to an end. The little duckling came out from behind his clump of weeds. Do you think he's changed?

As you wait for the audience to reply, take away the clump of weeds to reveal the new ugly duckling – a swan!

Ugly duckling

It's lovely to feel the sun on my feathers again.

Move the flying swans prop across the stage above the new ugly duckling.

My. Look at those beautiful white birds. I wish I could fly like them ... Hold on a minute ...

Ugly duckling

Rock the new ugly duckling as if he's trying his new wings out.

My wings seem so strong. I feel almost like a new bird ...

Ugly duckling

Hold the hand mirror for the new ugly duckling to look in. Hold it up so your audience can see what's happening.

Ugly duckling

Let me look at myself in the pond ...

Make the new ugly duckling jump around excitedly on stage.

Ugly duckling

Wow! I'm a swan! I'm a swan, I'm a swan!

Puppeteer

Sure enough, the ugly duckling had turned into a beautiful swan. Nobody teased him any more.

Stick the dog, cat and chicken puppets up one by one to speak to the new ugly duckling.

Dog

I'm sorry I was so rude. Woof, woof.

Cat

You're welcome to visit me any time. Meow.

Chicken

I wish I looked as good as you! Cluck, cluck.

Put your head up to talk to the audience,
with the new ugly duckling by your side.

Puppeteer

You see, it's wise not to tease someone who looks different. In fact, it's best not to tease anyone at all. Don't you agree?

Ugly duckling

Quack, quack!

THE END